MINDSET

Securing Your Legacy: A Guide to Life Insurance for Men and Women

Ray T Rose

Table of Contents

Chapter 1: Understanding Life Insurance Basics

Introduction to Life Insurance

Life insurance is a crucial financial tool that
provides protection and peace of mind for

individuals and their loved ones. In this subchapter, we will delve into the fundamentals of life insurance, exploring different types of policies and their benefits. Whether you are a man or a woman, understanding the basics of life insurance is essential for securing your legacy and ensuring financial stability for your family.

Life insurance serves as a safety net, offering financial support to your loved ones in the event of your untimely demise. It provides a lump sum payment, known as the death benefit, to your beneficiaries upon your passing. This money can be used to cover funeral expenses, outstanding debts, mortgage payments, or any other financial obligations your family may face.

There are several types of life insurance policies available to cater to different needs. One of the most common options is term life insurance, which provides coverage for a specified period, such as 10, 20, or 30 years. Term life insurance is ideal for individuals who require coverage for a specific period, such as when raising children, paying off a mortgage, or starting a business.

Another popular option is whole life insurance, which provides coverage for the entire duration of your life. Whole life insurance not only offers a death benefit but also accumulates cash value over time. This cash value can be accessed through policy loans or withdrawals, providing a source of funding for emergencies or retirement.

For those who want to ensure their final expenses are taken care of, burial insurance or final expense insurance is an ideal choice. These policies are specifically designed to cover funeral costs, medical bills, and other end-of-life expenses. With burial insurance, you can relieve your loved ones of the financial burden associated with your passing.

In this subchapter, we will explore the intricacies of each type of life insurance policy, discussing their advantages, drawbacks, and how to choose the right one for your needs. We will also address common misconceptions about life insurance and provide tips on how to maximize the benefits of your policy.

By the end of this subchapter, you will have a comprehensive understanding of life insurance and how it can secure your legacy. Whether you are seeking coverage for yourself or your family, this knowledge will empower you to make informed decisions and protect your loved ones financially.

Importance of Life Insurance for Men and Women

Life insurance is a crucial aspect of financial planning that should not be overlooked by anyone, regardless of gender. In the book "Securing Your

Legacy: A Guide to Life Insurance for Men and Women," we delve into the significance of life insurance for both men and women, and highlight the different types of coverage available to cater to specific needs.

For both men and women, life insurance serves as a safety net that provides financial protection to loved ones in the event of the policyholder's death. It ensures that dependents are not burdened with the financial consequences of losing a primary breadwinner or caregiver. Life insurance proceeds can be used to cover daily living expenses, mortgage payments, outstanding debts, education costs, and even funeral expenses.

When it comes to life insurance, there are several types of coverage to consider, depending on individual circumstances and financial goals. Term life insurance, for instance, offers coverage for a specific period, typically ranging from 10 to 30 years. This type of policy is suitable for individuals who want temporary coverage to protect their loved ones during their working years or until certain financial obligations, such as mortgage payments or college tuition fees, are fulfilled.

On the other hand, whole life insurance provides coverage for the entire lifetime of the insured. This type of policy not only offers a death benefit but also accumulates cash value over time, which can be accessed during the policyholder's lifetime. Whole life insurance is ideal for those seeking long-term coverage and a savings component that can be utilized for emergencies, retirement income, or leaving a financial legacy.

Apart from term and whole life insurance, burial insurance and final expense insurance are specialized policies designed to cover funeral and end-of-life expenses. These policies ensure that the policyholder's family is not burdened with the significant costs associated with a funeral, burial, or cremation.

In conclusion, life insurance is of utmost importance for both men and women. It provides financial security and peace of mind, ensuring that loved ones are protected and can maintain their quality of life in the face of a tragedy. Whether considering term life insurance, whole life insurance, burial insurance, or final expense insurance, it is essential to carefully evaluate individual needs and consult a trusted insurance professional to determine the most suitable coverage for your circumstances.

Types of Life Insurance Policies

Life insurance is a crucial financial tool that offers protection and peace of mind for individuals and their families in times of uncertainty. With numerous options available in the market, it's essential to understand the various types of life insurance policies to make an informed decision. This subchapter aims to provide an overview of the different types of life insurance policies, including term life insurance, whole life insurance, burial insurance, and final expense insurance.

Term life insurance is a popular choice among individuals seeking temporary coverage for a specific period, such as 10, 20, or 30 years. It offers a death benefit to the beneficiary if the insured passes away during the term of the policy. Term life insurance policies are typically affordable, making them an attractive option for young families or those with financial constraints.

On the other hand, whole life insurance provides lifelong coverage and includes a cash value component that grows over time. This policy type not only offers a death benefit but also accumulates cash value that can be borrowed against or withdrawn to supplement retirement income or cover unexpected expenses. Whole life insurance is often considered a long-term investment and offers more stability and financial security.

Burial insurance, also known as final expense insurance, is designed to cover funeral and burial expenses. It is a smaller policy that provides a specific death benefit to help alleviate the financial burden on loved ones during a difficult time. Burial insurance policies are generally easier to qualify for and have lower premiums compared to other types of life insurance.

Final expense insurance, similar to burial insurance, helps cover the costs associated with end-of-life expenses. It offers a modest death benefit to cover funeral costs, outstanding medical bills, and other outstanding debts. This type of policy is particularly useful for individuals who are unable to obtain traditional life insurance due to health issues or advanced age.

Understanding the various types of life insurance policies allows individuals to select the one that best suits their needs and circumstances. Whether it's term life insurance for temporary coverage, whole life insurance for lifelong protection and financial growth, or burial and final expense insurance for specific end-of-life expenses, there is a life insurance policy tailored to meet every individual's unique requirements.

Securing Your Legacy: A Guide to Life Insurance for Men and Women provides comprehensive information on these policies to help readers make informed decisions about their financial future and protect their loved ones in the face of uncertainty.

Chapter 2: Exploring Term Life Insurance

What is Term Life Insurance?

In the world of life insurance, there are various options available, each designed to cater to different needs and preferences. One such option is term life insurance, which has gained immense popularity in recent years. In this subchapter, we will delve into the intricacies of term life insurance, shedding light on its features, benefits, and suitability for both men and women.

Term life insurance is a type of life insurance coverage that provides protection for a specified period, typically ranging from 10 to 30 years. Unlike other forms of life insurance, term life insurance does not accumulate cash value over time. Instead, it acts as pure protection, ensuring that your loved ones receive a death benefit if you pass away during the policy term.

One of the key advantages of term life insurance is its affordability. The premiums for term life insurance policies are generally lower compared to whole life insurance or other permanent coverage options. This makes term life insurance an attractive choice for individuals who wish to secure their family's financial future without breaking the bank.

Term life insurance is ideal for those who have specific financial obligations that will decrease or disappear over time. For instance, if you have children and want to ensure their education expenses are covered until they become financially independent, a term life insurance policy can provide the necessary protection. Similarly, if you have outstanding debts such as a mortgage or loans, term life insurance can help ensure those debts are paid off in the event of your untimely demise.

Both men and women can benefit from term life insurance. For men, it can serve as a crucial financial safety net for their families, providing peace of mind that their loved ones will be taken care of even if they are no longer around. Women, who often play multiple roles within a family, can also find term life insurance invaluable. It can help cover childcare expenses, mortgage payments, or any other financial responsibilities that may arise in their absence.

In summary, term life insurance is a flexible and cost-effective option that offers temporary coverage for a specified period. Whether you are a man or a woman, term life insurance can provide the financial security your loved ones need in case of your unexpected departure. Understanding the features and benefits of term life insurance is essential in making informed decisions about securing your legacy and protecting your family's future.

Benefits of Term Life Insurance

Term life insurance is a type of life insurance policy that provides coverage for a specific period, typically ranging from 10 to 30 years. This subchapter aims to highlight the numerous benefits of term life insurance, addressing its relevance and advantages for both men and women.

One of the most significant benefits of term life insurance is its affordability. Compared to other types of life insurance policies, such as whole life insurance or burial insurance, term life insurance offers a more cost-effective option. This makes it an ideal choice for individuals who are looking for temporary coverage to protect their loved ones during specific stages of life, such as paying off a mortgage or providing for children's education.

Another advantage of term life insurance is its flexibility. Policyholders have the freedom to choose the coverage period that best suits their needs. For example, a young couple planning to start a family may opt for a 20-year term policy to ensure their children are financially secure until they reach adulthood. This flexibility allows individuals to align their coverage with their specific life goals and circumstances.

Additionally, term life insurance provides a death benefit to the beneficiaries if the insured passes away during the policy term. This benefit can be used to cover various expenses, such as mortgage payments, outstanding debts, funeral costs, or even provide a financial cushion for the family's future.

Term life insurance also offers the option to convert to a permanent life insurance policy. This feature can be beneficial for individuals who initially choose term life insurance due to its affordability but later decide they want lifelong coverage. Converting to a permanent policy ensures that individuals can maintain coverage beyond the initial term without the need for a new medical examination.

Moreover, term life insurance can provide peace of mind, knowing that loved ones will be financially protected in the event of an unforeseen tragedy. It offers a sense of security, allowing individuals to focus on their day-to-day lives without worrying about the financial burden their loved ones may face in their absence.

In conclusion, term life insurance offers several significant benefits for both men and women. Its affordability, flexibility, death benefit, conversion options, and peace of mind make it a valuable tool for securing the financial future of your loved ones during specific stages of life. Whether you are a young professional starting a family or an individual looking to protect your legacy, term life insurance can provide the necessary coverage and financial security to ensure your loved ones are well taken care of.

Factors to Consider When Choosing Term Life Insurance

When it comes to securing your legacy and protecting the financial well-being of your loved ones, term life insurance can be an excellent choice. This type of coverage offers a straightforward and affordable solution that provides a death benefit for a specified period, typically ranging from 10 to 30 years. However, with a multitude of options available in the market, it is crucial to consider several factors before selecting the right term life insurance policy for your needs.

Firstly, it is essential to determine the amount of coverage you require. Consider your financial obligations, such as mortgage payments, outstanding debts, and future educational expenses for your children. Assessing these factors will help you determine the appropriate death benefit that will adequately protect your family's financial future.

Secondly, take your age and health into account. Term life insurance premiums are primarily based on these factors, and the younger and healthier you are, the more affordable your premiums will be. It is advisable to obtain coverage while you are still young and in good health to lock in lower rates for the duration of the policy.

Furthermore, carefully evaluate the length of the term. Consider your family's long-term financial goals and obligations. If you have young children, a 20-year term policy may be suitable to ensure their financial stability until they become self-sufficient. On the other hand, if you have a mortgage or other long-term debts, a policy that aligns with the repayment timeline may be more suitable.

It is also crucial to consider the reputation and financial stability of the insurance company. Research and compare various insurers to ensure they have a solid track record of meeting their obligations and providing excellent customer service. Additionally, consider reading customer reviews and seeking recommendations from trusted sources to gain insights into the company's reliability and responsiveness.

Lastly, make sure you understand the policy's limitations and exclusions. Review the terms and conditions carefully to determine any restrictions on coverage, such as exclusions for high-risk activities or pre-existing medical conditions. Understanding these details will help you choose a policy that aligns with your specific needs and provides comprehensive protection.

By considering these factors when choosing term life insurance, you can make an informed decision that secures your legacy and provides financial stability for your loved ones. Remember to regularly review and update your policy as your circumstances change to ensure continued protection and peace of mind.

Common Misconceptions about Term Life Insurance

In today's fast-paced world, it is crucial to secure your family's financial future. Life insurance plays a vital role in providing financial protection and peace of mind. However, there are several misconceptions surrounding term life insurance that often prevent people from making informed decisions. In this subchapter, we will debunk some of the most common misconceptions about term life insurance.

Misconception 1: Term life insurance is unnecessary if you are young and healthy.
Many individuals believe that life insurance is only for older people or those with health issues. However, the truth is that life is unpredictable, and accidents or illnesses can strike at any age. Term life insurance provides coverage for a specific

period, usually 10, 20, or 30 years, and can offer significant benefits even to young and healthy individuals.

Misconception 2: Term life insurance is too expensive.
Contrary to popular belief, term life insurance is generally more affordable compared to other types of life insurance such as whole life or universal life insurance. Since term life insurance provides coverage for a predetermined period, the premiums are often lower, making it a budget-friendly option for many individuals and families.

Misconception 3: Term life insurance only covers death benefits.
While it is true that term life insurance primarily provides death benefits to the policyholder's beneficiaries, some policies offer additional features. For instance, some term life insurance plans may include living benefits, allowing the policyholder to access a portion of the death benefit in case of a terminal illness or critical condition.

Misconception 4: Term life insurance is unnecessary if you have other insurance policies.
Having other insurance policies, such as health insurance or disability insurance, is essential, but they serve different purposes. Term life insurance provides a lump sum payment to your loved ones in the event of your untimely demise, ensuring their

financial stability and covering expenses such as mortgage payments, education costs, and daily living expenses.

Misconception 5: You can only purchase term life insurance through an agent.
While working with an insurance agent can provide valuable guidance, it is not the only way to purchase term life insurance. Nowadays, many reputable insurance companies offer online platforms that allow individuals to compare quotes, customize policies, and purchase term life insurance directly.

Understanding the truth behind these misconceptions is crucial for making informed decisions about term life insurance. It is important to consult with a licensed insurance professional to assess your specific needs and find the right term life insurance policy that aligns with your goals and budget. By securing your legacy through term life insurance, you can protect your loved ones and provide them with financial security when they need it the most.

Chapter 3: Unveiling Whole Life Insurance

What is Whole Life Insurance?

Whole life insurance is a type of life insurance policy that provides coverage for the entirety of your life, as long as you continue paying the premiums. Unlike term life insurance, which only provides coverage for a specific period, whole life insurance offers both a death benefit and a cash value component.

The death benefit is the amount of money that will be paid out to your beneficiaries upon your death. This financial protection ensures that your loved ones will have the necessary funds to cover funeral expenses, outstanding debts, and provide financial stability in your absence. The death benefit can be customized based on your needs and can range from a few thousand dollars to several million.

In addition to the death benefit, whole life insurance also accumulates a cash value over time. This cash value grows at a guaranteed rate and is tax-deferred, meaning you won't have to pay taxes on the growth until you withdraw it. You can access this cash value through loans or withdrawals, which can be a valuable source of funds for emergencies, education expenses, or supplemental retirement income.

One of the key advantages of whole life insurance is its permanent nature. As long as you continue paying the premiums, the policy remains in force for your entire life, regardless of any changes in your health or lifestyle. This stability and certainty make whole life insurance a reliable tool for estate planning and leaving a lasting legacy for your loved ones.

Whole life insurance also offers some unique benefits compared to other types of life insurance. For instance, it can serve as a savings vehicle, providing a guaranteed return on your premiums. Additionally, whole life insurance policies often come with a level premium, meaning the premium remains the same throughout the life of the policy, regardless of age or health changes.

In summary, whole life insurance provides lifelong coverage, a death benefit, and a cash value component that can be accessed during your lifetime. It offers stability, financial protection, and the ability to grow your wealth over time. Whether you are looking to secure your family's future, build an inheritance, or have a reliable savings plan, whole life insurance is a valuable tool to consider.

Advantages and Disadvantages of Whole Life Insurance

Whole life insurance is a type of permanent life insurance that offers both a death benefit and a cash value component. While it provides lifelong coverage, it also comes with its own set of advantages and disadvantages. In this subchapter, we will explore the benefits and drawbacks of whole life insurance, providing valuable insights for men, women, and individuals interested in life insurance, term life insurance, whole life insurance, burial insurance, and final expense insurance.

Advantages of Whole Life Insurance:
1. Lifelong Coverage: One of the significant advantages of whole life insurance is that it provides coverage for your entire life. As long as you pay your premiums, the death benefit will be paid out to your beneficiaries upon your passing, providing financial security and peace of mind.

2. Cash Value Growth: Whole life insurance builds cash value over time, which can be accessed during your lifetime. This accumulated cash value can be borrowed against or withdrawn to cover expenses such as education, emergencies, or supplementing retirement income.

3. Tax Advantages: The cash value growth within a whole life insurance policy is tax-deferred. This means you won't owe taxes on the growth until you withdraw or borrow against it. Additionally, the death benefit is generally tax-free for your beneficiaries.

Disadvantages of Whole Life Insurance:
1. Higher Premiums: Whole life insurance tends to have higher premiums compared to term life insurance. This is because it offers lifelong

coverage and builds cash value. The premiums for whole life insurance may be a financial burden for some individuals.

2. Limited Flexibility: Unlike term life insurance, whole life insurance does not offer as much flexibility. Once you choose a policy, you may be locked into paying premiums for the rest of your life, even if your financial circumstances change.

3. Lower Returns: The cash value growth in a whole life insurance policy is typically lower compared to other investment options, such as stocks or mutual funds. If your primary goal is to maximize investment returns, other investment vehicles may be more suitable.

In conclusion, whole life insurance offers lifelong coverage, cash value growth, and tax advantages. However, it comes with higher premiums, limited flexibility, and potentially lower returns. It is essential to carefully consider your financial goals and needs before deciding if whole life insurance aligns with your objectives.

Understanding Cash Value and Dividends in Whole Life Insurance

Whole life insurance is a type of permanent life insurance that offers lifelong coverage along with a cash value component and potential dividends. It provides a unique combination of insurance protection and savings, making it an attractive option for individuals looking to secure their legacy and provide financial security for their loved ones.

Cash value is one of the key features of whole life insurance. As you pay your premiums, a portion of the money goes towards the cost of insurance coverage, while the rest is invested by the insurance company. Over time, the cash value grows tax-deferred, meaning you won't have to pay taxes on the growth until you withdraw it.

The cash value can be used in a variety of ways. You can borrow against it, using it as collateral for a loan, or you can withdraw a portion of it to supplement your retirement income or cover unexpected expenses. It can also be used to pay your premiums if you find yourself in a financial bind. However, it's important to note that any loans or withdrawals will reduce the death benefit your beneficiaries receive.

Dividends, on the other hand, are not guaranteed but can be a valuable feature of whole life insurance policies. When an insurance company performs well and generates excess profits, it may distribute a portion of those profits to policyholders in the form of dividends. These dividends can be used in several ways, such as reducing premiums, purchasing additional coverage, or accumulating interest.

Understanding the cash value and dividends in whole life insurance is essential for making informed decisions about your policy. It's important to review your policy annually and consult with your insurance agent to assess the performance of your policy and explore any potential opportunities for utilizing the cash value or maximizing dividends.

For men and women considering life insurance, whole life insurance offers a comprehensive solution that not only provides a death benefit but also builds cash value and offers the potential for dividends. Whether you are looking for coverage to protect your family, plan for your retirement, or ensure your final expenses are covered, whole life insurance can help you secure your legacy and provide peace of mind for yourself and your loved ones.

In conclusion, whole life insurance is a versatile and valuable tool that combines insurance protection with savings and investment opportunities. By understanding the cash value and dividends associated with whole life insurance, you can make informed decisions about your policy and customize it to meet your specific needs and goals.

How to Determine If Whole Life Insurance is Right for You

Life insurance is an essential financial tool that provides protection and peace of mind for you and your loved ones. With various types of life insurance policies available, it can be overwhelming to choose the right one for your specific needs. In this subchapter, we will focus on whole life insurance and help you determine if it is the right option for you.

Whole life insurance is a type of permanent life insurance that offers lifelong coverage and includes a cash value component. Unlike term life insurance, which provides coverage for a specific period, whole life insurance ensures that your loved ones are financially protected regardless of when you pass away.

Before deciding if whole life insurance is the right fit for you, it is crucial to consider your financial goals and needs. Here are some factors to evaluate:

1. Long-term financial planning: Whole life insurance is an excellent choice if you want to leave a financial legacy to your loved ones or have specific long-term financial goals, such as funding your child's education or passing on wealth to future generations.

2. Permanent coverage: If you want the peace of mind of knowing that your life insurance coverage will never expire, whole life insurance is the right option. It guarantees a death benefit payout to your beneficiaries, regardless of when you pass away.

3. Accumulating cash value: Whole life insurance policies accumulate cash value over time, which you can access through policy loans or withdrawals. If you are looking for a life insurance policy that can provide both protection and savings, whole life insurance may be the right choice.

4. Affordability: While whole life insurance offers lifelong coverage, it tends to have higher premium costs compared to term life insurance. Evaluate your budget and ensure that the premiums are affordable for the long term.

5. Estate planning: If you have substantial assets and want to ensure a smooth transfer of wealth to your beneficiaries, whole life insurance can be a valuable tool in your estate planning strategy.

Ultimately, the decision to choose whole life insurance depends on your individual circumstances and financial goals. It is essential to consult with a trusted life insurance professional who can assess your needs and help you make an informed decision.

Remember, securing your legacy is of utmost importance, and by understanding the benefits and considerations of whole life insurance, you can ensure that you are making the right choice for your financial future and the well-being of your loved ones.

Chapter 4: Navigating Burial Insurance

What is Burial Insurance?

When it comes to planning for the future, one aspect that often gets overlooked is the financial burden of end-of-life expenses. Many men and women are unaware of the potential costs associated with burial and funeral services, leaving their loved ones to bear the burden. This is where burial insurance comes into play.

Burial insurance, also known as final expense insurance, is a type of life insurance specifically designed to cover the expenses related to funerals, burials, and other end-of-life costs. It provides a financial safety net to ensure that your family is not left with the heavy burden of paying for your funeral arrangements.

Unlike other types of life insurance policies, burial insurance typically offers lower coverage amounts, ranging from a few thousand dollars to around $25,000. This makes it an affordable option for individuals who are primarily concerned with covering their final expenses rather than leaving a large sum of money as a legacy.

One of the key benefits of burial insurance is its simplicity. It is relatively easy to qualify for, as most policies do not require a medical exam or extensive underwriting. This makes it an attractive option for individuals who may have pre-existing health conditions or are older in age.

Another advantage of burial insurance is the quick payout. Unlike traditional life insurance policies that may take weeks or even months to process, burial insurance policies often pay out within a few days, providing immediate financial support to your loved ones during a difficult time.

It is important, however, to carefully consider your options and choose a reputable insurance provider. Research different policies, compare rates, and read customer reviews to ensure that you are getting the best coverage at the most competitive price.

In conclusion, burial insurance is a valuable financial tool that can help alleviate the financial burden of end-of-life expenses for your loved ones. By planning ahead and securing burial insurance coverage, you can have peace of mind knowing that your final expenses will be taken care of, allowing your family to focus on grieving and healing rather than worrying about financial obligations.

Why Burial Insurance is Important for Men and Women

In the realm of life insurance, there are various types of policies available to suit different needs and circumstances. Among these, burial insurance holds a significant place, particularly for both men and women. In this subchapter, we will explore why burial insurance is an essential consideration for individuals seeking financial security and peace of mind.

Burial insurance, also known as final expense insurance, is designed to cover the costs associated with end-of-life expenses, such as funeral and burial expenses, medical bills, outstanding debts, and other related costs. While no one likes to think about their own mortality, it is a reality that we must all face. By obtaining burial insurance, individuals can ensure that their loved ones are not burdened with the financial implications that arise after their passing.

For men and women alike, burial insurance offers numerous advantages. Firstly, it provides a level of financial security for loved ones left behind. Funeral and burial costs can be substantial, often ranging from several thousand to tens of thousands of dollars, depending on individual preferences and regional factors. By having burial insurance in place, individuals can alleviate the financial burden on their families during a difficult time, allowing them to focus on grieving and healing.

Furthermore, burial insurance offers a simple and accessible solution for individuals who may have difficulty obtaining traditional life insurance policies. Factors such as age, health conditions, or lifestyle choices can sometimes present obstacles when seeking life insurance. However, burial insurance typically has more lenient underwriting requirements, making it a viable option for those who may have been declined for other types of coverage.

Another crucial aspect of burial insurance is its flexibility. Policyholders have the freedom to choose the coverage amount that best fits their needs, ensuring that their final expenses are adequately covered. This allows individuals to customize their policies based on their unique circumstances, providing the peace of mind that their wishes will be fulfilled and their loved ones will not face financial hardship.

In conclusion, burial insurance is an essential consideration for both men and women when planning for their financial legacy. By securing this type of coverage, individuals can ensure that their loved ones are not burdened with the financial strain that often accompanies end-of-life expenses. Burial insurance offers a simple and accessible solution, providing financial security and peace of mind. By exploring the benefits and options available, individuals can make informed decisions about their life insurance needs, ultimately securing their legacy for future generations.

Selecting the Right Burial Insurance Plan

When it comes to planning for the inevitable, burial insurance is a crucial component that often gets overlooked. While no one likes to think about their own mortality, it is essential to ensure that your loved ones are not burdened with hefty funeral costs when the time comes. In this subchapter, we will discuss the importance of selecting the right burial insurance plan and provide you with valuable insights to help you make an informed decision.

Burial insurance, also known as final expense insurance, is specifically designed to cover funeral expenses, outstanding debts, and other end-of-life costs. Unlike traditional life insurance policies, burial insurance offers smaller coverage amounts, typically ranging from $5,000 to $25,000, which makes it more affordable and accessible for individuals seeking to secure their legacy.

When selecting the right burial insurance plan, it is crucial to consider several factors. First and foremost, determine the coverage amount you need. Assess your funeral costs, outstanding debts, and any other potential expenses that your loved ones may face after your passing. This will give you a clear idea of how much coverage you require to alleviate their financial burden.

Next, evaluate the different types of burial insurance plans available. The two main options are term life insurance and whole life insurance. Term life insurance provides coverage for a specific period, typically 10 to 30 years, while whole life insurance offers lifelong coverage. Consider your age, health condition, and financial situation to determine which option is best suited for you.

Furthermore, compare multiple burial insurance providers and their policies. Look for reputable companies with a proven track record in the life insurance industry. Consider their customer reviews, financial stability, and claim settlement process. It is also essential to review the policy's terms and conditions, including any potential exclusions or limitations, to ensure it aligns with your specific needs.

Finally, consult with an experienced life insurance agent or financial advisor. They can provide expert guidance and help you navigate the complexities of burial insurance. They will assess your unique circumstances and offer personalized recommendations to ensure you select the right burial insurance plan.

In conclusion, securing the right burial insurance plan is a critical step in protecting your loved ones from financial hardship during an already challenging time. By considering the coverage amount, type of policy, and reputable providers, you can make an informed decision that provides peace of mind for both you and your family. Remember, burial insurance is not just about securing your legacy – it's about ensuring that your loved ones can properly honor and remember you without the added burden of financial strain.

Final Expense Planning with Burial Insurance

When it comes to planning for the future, one aspect that often gets overlooked is final expense planning. Many individuals fail to realize that funeral and burial costs can be a significant financial burden on their loved ones. This is where burial insurance, also known as final expense insurance, comes into play. In this subchapter, we will explore the importance of final expense planning and how burial insurance can provide peace of mind for both men and women.

Final expense planning is the process of preparing for the costs associated with one's funeral, burial, and other end-of-life expenses. While it may seem morbid to think about, it is an essential part of financial planning. By taking the time to plan ahead, individuals can ensure that their final wishes are met, and their loved ones are not burdened with the financial stress during an already challenging time.

Burial insurance is a type of life insurance specifically designed to cover the costs of funeral and burial expenses. Unlike other types of life insurance, burial insurance offers a smaller death benefit, typically ranging from $5,000 to $25,000. This lower coverage amount ensures that the policy remains affordable and accessible for individuals who may not require a larger life insurance policy.

For men and women, burial insurance provides a sense of security knowing that their loved ones will not be left with the financial responsibility of their funeral expenses. It allows individuals to plan their final arrangements in advance, ensuring that their wishes are carried out and relieving their loved ones of the burden of making difficult decisions during a time of grief.

Additionally, burial insurance is often easier to obtain compared to other types of life insurance. It typically requires minimal underwriting, making it an attractive option for individuals who may have health conditions that could disqualify them from traditional life insurance policies. This accessibility makes burial insurance an ideal choice for those seeking a simple and affordable solution to their final expense planning needs.

In conclusion, final expense planning is a crucial aspect of overall financial planning. By considering the costs associated with one's funeral and burial, individuals can relieve their loved ones of the financial burden during an already challenging time. Burial insurance offers an accessible and affordable solution for men and women who want to ensure their final wishes are met and their loved ones are taken care of.

Chapter 5: Decoding Final Expense Insurance

Understanding Final Expense Insurance

Final expense insurance, also known as burial insurance, is a specific type of life insurance that is designed to cover the costs associated with a person's funeral, burial, and other end-of-life expenses. This type of insurance policy is particularly important for individuals who do not have a significant amount of savings or assets that can be used to cover these expenses.

One of the key advantages of final expense insurance is that it provides peace of mind and financial security to both the policyholder and their loved ones. By having this type of insurance coverage, individuals can ensure that their funeral expenses will be taken care of without burdening their family members with the financial responsibilities during a difficult time.

Final expense insurance policies are typically smaller in face value compared to other types of life insurance policies. The coverage amount can range from a few thousand dollars up to around $25,000, depending on the individual's needs and budget. The funds from the policy are usually paid out quickly after the policyholder's death, providing immediate financial assistance to cover funeral costs and other related expenses.

One of the key benefits of final expense insurance is that it is relatively easy to qualify for, especially compared to other types of life insurance policies. These policies typically do not require a medical exam, making them more accessible for individuals who may have pre-existing health conditions or who are older in age. Additionally, the premiums for final expense insurance are often more affordable compared to other types of life insurance, making it an attractive option for those on a limited budget.

When considering final expense insurance, it is important to carefully review and compare different policies to ensure that you are getting the right coverage for your needs. Factors to consider include the face value of the policy, the premium amounts, and any additional benefits or riders that may be included.

In conclusion, final expense insurance is a valuable type of coverage that provides financial security and peace of mind for both the policyholder and their loved ones. It ensures that funeral and burial expenses are taken care of and relieves the financial burden on family members during a difficult time. By understanding the benefits and features of final expense insurance, individuals can make informed decisions to secure their legacy and protect their loved ones after their passing.

Benefits and Features of Final Expense Insurance

In this subchapter, we will delve into the myriad of benefits and features that Final Expense Insurance offers to both men and women. Final Expense Insurance, also known as burial insurance or funeral insurance, is a specialized type of life insurance that is designed to cover the costs associated with end-of-life expenses. It provides financial security and peace of mind for individuals and their loved ones during a challenging and emotional time.

One of the primary benefits of Final Expense Insurance is its affordability. Unlike traditional life insurance policies, Final Expense Insurance is typically available at lower premium rates. This makes it accessible to a wider range of individuals, including those who may have difficulty qualifying for other types of coverage due to age or health conditions. Regardless of your current health status, there are often options available that can meet your specific needs.

Another key advantage of Final Expense Insurance is its simplicity. The application process is typically straightforward and requires minimal medical underwriting. This means that you can secure coverage quickly and easily, without the need for extensive paperwork or medical examinations. This simplicity makes it an ideal choice for individuals who are seeking immediate coverage or who have been previously denied coverage due to health issues.

Additionally, Final Expense Insurance provides a lump-sum payout to your designated beneficiary upon your passing. This payout can be used to cover funeral expenses, medical bills, outstanding debts, or any other costs associated with your final arrangements. By securing this coverage, you can alleviate the financial burden on your loved ones during an already difficult time, ensuring that they can focus on grieving and healing, rather than worrying about financial obligations.

Furthermore, Final Expense Insurance offers the flexibility to choose a coverage amount that suits your specific needs. Whether you require a small policy to cover funeral expenses or a larger policy to address outstanding debts or estate taxes, there are a variety of options available to tailor the coverage to your unique situation.

In conclusion, Final Expense Insurance provides numerous benefits and features that make it a valuable option for both men and women. Its affordability, simplicity, and flexibility make it an accessible choice for individuals seeking to secure their legacy and protect their loved ones from the financial burden of end-of-life expenses. By considering Final Expense Insurance, you can ensure that your final wishes are honored and your family's financial well-being is safeguarded.

How to Choose the Best Final Expense Insurance Policy

When it comes to planning for the future, one aspect that often gets overlooked is final expense insurance. Final expense insurance, also known as burial insurance, is designed to cover the costs associated with end-of-life expenses, such as funeral and burial costs. It is an important consideration for both men and women, regardless of age or health.

Choosing the best final expense insurance policy can be a daunting task, given the wide range of options available in the market. However, with the right knowledge and guidance, you can make an informed decision that will provide financial security for your loved ones during a difficult time.

Firstly, it is essential to understand the different types of final expense insurance policies available. The most common options are term life insurance and whole life insurance. Term life insurance provides coverage for a specific period, usually 10 to 30 years, while whole life insurance offers lifelong coverage. Burial insurance is a type of whole life insurance specifically designed to cover funeral and burial expenses.

When selecting a final expense insurance policy, consider your specific needs and circumstances. Assess your financial situation, including any outstanding debts or mortgage payments, to determine the coverage amount required. Take into account the average cost of funerals in your area, as prices can vary significantly.

Another crucial factor to consider is your health condition. Some final expense insurance policies require a medical exam, while others offer guaranteed acceptance regardless of health status. Keep in mind that policies without medical exams may have higher premiums.

Researching and comparing different insurance providers is also essential. Look for reputable companies with a track record of excellent customer service and financial stability. Read reviews and seek recommendations from friends, family, or financial advisors familiar with the life insurance industry.

Additionally, carefully review the policy details, including the premium amount, payment frequency, and any additional riders or benefits offered. Some policies may allow for cash value accumulation, which can be useful for unexpected expenses during your lifetime.

In conclusion, choosing the best final expense insurance policy requires careful consideration of your specific needs and circumstances. Take the time to research different types of policies, assess your financial situation, and compare various insurance providers. By doing so, you can secure the financial future of your loved ones and ensure peace of mind during a challenging time.

Comparing Final Expense Insurance Options for Men and Women

When it comes to planning for the future, one crucial aspect that often gets overlooked is final expense insurance. This type of insurance is specifically designed to cover the costs associated with end-of-life expenses, such as funeral and burial costs. However, it is essential to understand that the options available for men and women may differ due to various factors.

The first thing to consider is life expectancy. Statistically, women tend to live longer than men. Therefore, insurance companies may calculate the premiums differently based on gender. Men may be subject to higher premiums due to their shorter life expectancy. It is essential to take this into account when comparing final expense insurance options.

Another factor to consider is the coverage amount. Final expense insurance typically offers coverage that ranges from a few thousand dollars to tens of thousands of dollars. The coverage amount should be chosen based on individual needs and the expected expenses. For instance, women may want to consider higher coverage due to the fact that they tend to live longer, thereby potentially incurring more end-of-life expenses.

Additionally, the type of final expense insurance should also be compared. There are several options available, including term life insurance, whole life insurance, burial insurance, and final expense insurance. Term life insurance provides coverage for a specific period, while whole life insurance offers coverage for the entire lifetime. Burial insurance and final expense insurance are specifically designed to cover funeral and burial costs. Each option has its advantages, and individuals should carefully evaluate which one aligns best with their needs.

Furthermore, it is crucial to consider the financial stability and reputation of the insurance company. When comparing final expense insurance options, it is essential to choose a reputable company that has a history of prompt claim settlements and excellent customer service. Researching customer reviews and ratings can provide valuable insights into the company's reliability.

In conclusion, comparing final expense insurance options for men and women requires careful consideration of factors such as life expectancy, coverage amount, and the type of insurance. It is crucial to choose an option that meets individual needs and provides financial security for loved ones after one's passing. By understanding the differences between options and conducting thorough research, both men and women can secure their legacies and provide peace of mind for their families.

Chapter 6: Maximizing Life Insurance Benefits

Tips for Maximizing Life Insurance Coverage

When it comes to securing your future and protecting your loved ones, life insurance is a crucial tool. However, choosing the right coverage and optimizing its benefits can often be overwhelming. This subchapter aims to provide valuable tips for men and women seeking to maximize their life insurance coverage, regardless of whether they are interested in term life insurance, whole life insurance, burial insurance, or final expense insurance.

1. Assess Your Needs: Before selecting a life insurance policy, evaluate your financial situation, obligations, and long-term goals. Consider factors such as mortgage payments, outstanding debts, educational expenses, and income replacement. This assessment will help you determine the appropriate coverage amount and policy type.

2. Understand Policy Types: Familiarize yourself with the different types of life insurance policies available. Term life insurance offers coverage for a specified period, while whole life insurance

provides lifelong protection. Burial insurance and final expense insurance are specialized policies that cover funeral costs and other end-of-life expenses. Understanding the nuances of each policy type will enable you to make an informed decision.

3. Work with an Expert: Seek guidance from a reputable life insurance agent or financial advisor. These professionals can evaluate your needs, explain policy options, and help you navigate the complexities of the insurance market. Their expertise will ensure that you secure the most suitable coverage for your circumstances.

4. Shop Around: Compare quotes from multiple insurance providers to find the best policy at the most affordable rate. Different insurers offer varying premiums, coverage options, and benefits. Take advantage of online resources and request quotes from several companies to make an informed choice.

5. Review Regularly: Life circumstances change over time, so it's important to regularly review your life insurance coverage. Major life events such as marriage, having children, or purchasing a home may require adjustments to your policy. Reviewing your coverage annually or after significant life changes will help ensure that your loved ones are adequately protected.

By following these tips, men and women can maximize their life insurance coverage and provide financial security for their families. Remember, life insurance is not a one-size-fits-all solution, and it's essential to tailor your coverage to your specific needs. Take the time to understand the options available, consult with experts, and regularly reassess your policy to ensure it aligns with your changing circumstances.

Strategies to Ensure Your Life Insurance Policy Meets Your Needs

When it comes to life insurance, it's crucial to select a policy that aligns with your specific needs. Whether you are a man or a woman, understanding the various types of life insurance available to you can greatly impact the level of financial security you provide for your loved ones. In this subchapter, we will explore effective strategies to ensure your life insurance policy meets your unique requirements.

1. Assessing Your Needs: The first step in securing the right life insurance policy is evaluating your financial status, future goals, and responsibilities. Consider factors such as mortgage payments, outstanding debts, educational expenses, and the financial needs of your dependents. This assessment will help determine the appropriate

coverage amount and type of life insurance that suits your circumstances.

2. Understanding the Types of Life Insurance: Life insurance comes in several forms, including term life insurance, whole life insurance, burial insurance, and final expense insurance. Each type has its advantages and disadvantages, making it essential to understand how they differ and which one best fits your needs. Term life insurance provides coverage for a specific period, while whole life insurance offers lifelong protection with cash value accumulation. Burial and final expense insurance are designed to cover end-of-life expenses, ensuring your loved ones are not burdened with funeral costs.

3. Consulting with an Insurance Professional: Seeking guidance from an experienced insurance professional is paramount in selecting the right policy. They can provide invaluable advice, assess your needs accurately, and recommend the most suitable coverage options within your budget. These professionals have in-depth knowledge of the insurance market and can help you navigate through the complexities of policies, ensuring you make an informed decision.

4. Regular Policy Reviews: Life is dynamic, and so are your financial circumstances. Periodic policy reviews are essential to ensure your coverage

remains adequate as your life evolves. Life events such as marriage, birth of a child, or a career change may necessitate adjustments to your life insurance policy. By conducting regular policy reviews, you can ensure that your coverage aligns with your changing needs.

5. Consider Riders and Additional Coverage: Riders are optional add-ons to your life insurance policy that provide additional benefits. These can include critical illness riders, disability income riders, or accelerated death benefit riders. Assess your needs and consider adding riders to your policy to enhance your coverage and offer extra protection in times of need.

By employing these strategies, both men and women can secure a life insurance policy that not only meets their current needs but also provides long-term financial security for their loved ones. Remember, life insurance is not a one-size-fits-all solution, so take the time to evaluate your needs, consult with professionals, and regularly review your policy to ensure it remains effective throughout your lifetime.

Planning for Future Generations with Life Insurance

Life insurance is not just about protecting yourself; it is also about planning for your loved ones and future generations. By securing a life insurance policy, you can ensure financial stability for your family, leave a lasting legacy, and provide for the needs of future generations. In this subchapter, we will explore the various ways life insurance can help you plan for the future and the different types of policies available to suit your needs.

When it comes to securing your legacy, life insurance is a crucial tool. It allows you to leave behind a financial safety net for your loved ones, ensuring they are taken care of even after you are gone. Life insurance can replace lost income, pay off debts, cover funeral expenses, and fund your children's education. By having a well-thought-out life insurance plan, you can provide your family with the resources they need to maintain their standard of living and achieve their goals.

There are several types of life insurance policies to consider when planning for your future and the needs of future generations. Term life insurance provides coverage for a specific period, typically 10, 20, or 30 years. It is an affordable option that offers a high death benefit, making it ideal for young families who want to ensure their children's financial security.

Whole life insurance, on the other hand, offers lifelong coverage and also builds cash value over time. It provides a death benefit and serves as a savings vehicle, which can be accessed during your lifetime for various needs, such as funding your retirement or helping your children with their own financial goals.

For those specifically looking to cover final expenses, burial insurance or final expense insurance is an excellent choice. These policies are designed to pay for funeral costs, medical bills, and outstanding debts, relieving your loved ones of the financial burden during an already challenging time.

Regardless of which type of life insurance you choose, the important thing is to plan ahead and consider the needs of your family and future generations. Life insurance is a proactive step that can provide peace of mind knowing that your loved ones will be taken care of, and your legacy will be secured.

In conclusion, planning for future generations with life insurance is a fundamental aspect of financial planning. It allows you to leave behind a lasting legacy, provide financial security for your family, and ensure your loved ones can achieve their dreams. Whether you opt for term life insurance, whole life insurance, burial insurance, or final expense insurance, the key is to take action and secure your family's future today.

Common Life Insurance Mistakes to Avoid

Life insurance is an essential tool for securing the financial future of your loved ones. It provides peace of mind knowing that they will be protected in the event of your untimely demise. However, navigating the world of life insurance can be complex, and making mistakes along the way can have significant consequences. In this subchapter, we will discuss some common life insurance mistakes to avoid, providing valuable insights for both men and women seeking to secure their legacy.

One of the most common mistakes people make is underestimating their coverage needs. When determining the amount of life insurance to purchase, it is crucial to consider all financial obligations, including mortgages, debts, education expenses, and daily living costs. Failing to account for these factors may leave your loved ones struggling to make ends meet after your passing.

Another critical mistake is not reviewing your life insurance policy regularly. Life circumstances change, and your insurance coverage should reflect those changes. Whether it's a marriage, the birth of a child, or a promotion at work, these milestones can impact your coverage needs. Regularly reviewing your policy ensures that it remains aligned with your current financial situation.

Furthermore, many individuals overlook the significance of comparing different insurance policies and providers. Each type of life insurance, be it term life, whole life, burial, or final expense insurance, has its unique features and benefits. By not considering all available options, you may miss out on more affordable premiums or additional coverage features that suit your needs.

Additionally, failing to disclose accurate information on your life insurance application can lead to complications down the line. It is crucial to provide honest and thorough information about your health, lifestyle, and any pre-existing conditions. Failing to do so may result in claim denials or increased premiums, undermining the very purpose of life insurance.

Lastly, procrastination is a common mistake many make when it comes to life insurance. Delaying the purchase of a policy can be risky, as life is unpredictable, and waiting too long may lead to increased premiums or potential health issues that could make you uninsurable. It is wise to start planning for life insurance as early as possible.

By avoiding these common life insurance mistakes, you can ensure that your loved ones are adequately protected in the future. Remember to assess your coverage needs accurately, review your policy regularly, compare different options, provide accurate information, and start planning early. With these tips in mind, you can secure your legacy and provide financial security for those who matter most.

Chapter 7: Planning for Your Legacy

The Role of Life Insurance in Legacy Planning

Legacy planning is an essential aspect of financial management that ensures your assets, values, and memories are passed down to future generations. While it may seem daunting, life insurance can play a significant role in simplifying and securing your legacy for both men and women.

Life insurance, in general, provides a financial safety net for your loved ones in the event of your untimely demise. It ensures that your family's financial obligations, such as mortgages, debts, and college tuition, are taken care of. However, life insurance goes beyond mere protection; it can be a powerful tool for legacy planning.

Term life insurance is a popular choice for individuals seeking affordable coverage for a specific period. By designating beneficiaries, you can secure your legacy by providing a financial cushion to loved ones after you're gone. This can be particularly crucial for men and women looking to leave an inheritance or ensure the financial stability of their family members.

Whole life insurance, on the other hand, offers lifelong coverage and includes a cash value component that grows over time. This cash value can be used to fund various aspects of your legacy plan, such as setting up trusts, endowments, or even charitable donations. By incorporating whole life insurance into your legacy planning, you can leave a lasting impact on causes that are close to your heart.

For those primarily concerned with covering end-of-life expenses, burial insurance or final expense insurance can provide peace of mind. These specialized types of life insurance policies ensure that funeral costs, medical bills, and other related expenses are taken care of, alleviating the financial burden on your loved ones during an already challenging time.

Regardless of the specific life insurance policy you choose, it's crucial to regularly review and update your coverage as your circumstances evolve. As men and women progress through different life stages, their legacy planning needs may change. Whether you get married, have children, or start a business, adjusting your life insurance coverage ensures that your legacy remains protected and aligned with your goals.

In conclusion, life insurance plays a vital role in legacy planning for both men and women. It provides financial security for your loved ones and allows you to leave a lasting impact on future generations. By understanding the various types of life insurance, such as term life, whole life, burial, or final expense insurance, individuals can tailor their legacy plan to their unique needs and aspirations. So, take the first step towards securing your legacy today by exploring the world of life insurance.

Incorporating Life Insurance into Estate Planning

Life insurance is a powerful tool that can provide financial security for your loved ones even after you are gone. It allows you to leave a legacy and ensure that your family members are taken care of in the event of your untimely demise. Integrating life insurance into your estate planning is a crucial step towards securing your legacy and protecting your family's future.

When it comes to life insurance, there are various options available to suit different needs. Term life insurance, whole life insurance, burial insurance, and final expense insurance are some of the common types that cater to specific situations. Each type has its benefits and features, making it essential to understand which one aligns best with your circumstances.

Term life insurance provides coverage for a specific term, usually ranging from 10 to 30 years. It offers a death benefit that can replace lost income, pay off debts, or fund your children's education. This type of insurance is ideal for those looking for coverage during their working years when financial responsibilities are high.

Whole life insurance, on the other hand, offers lifelong coverage with an investment component. It not only provides a death benefit but also accumulates cash value over time. This cash value can be used as a source of funds for emergencies, education, or retirement, making it a valuable asset in your estate planning.

Burial insurance and final expense insurance are specifically designed to cover funeral and end-of-life expenses. These policies ensure that your loved ones are not burdened with the financial stress of arranging a funeral or paying off outstanding debts after your passing.

Incorporating life insurance into your estate planning involves carefully evaluating your financial goals and obligations. It is essential to assess the amount of coverage you need to secure your family's financial future. Additionally, consider naming beneficiaries who will receive the proceeds from the policy and ensure that this aligns with your overall estate plan.

Consulting with a financial advisor or an estate planning attorney can be immensely beneficial when incorporating life insurance into your estate planning. They can guide you through the process, help you understand the tax implications, and ensure that your plan is tailored to your unique needs.

In conclusion, life insurance is a vital component of estate planning and can provide peace of mind knowing that your loved ones will be financially protected. By understanding the different types of life insurance available and seeking professional advice, you can create a comprehensive estate plan that secures your legacy for the benefit of your family. Whether you opt for term life insurance or whole life insurance, burial insurance, or final expense insurance, incorporating life insurance into your estate planning is an investment in your family's future.

Wealth Transfer Strategies Using Life Insurance

Life insurance is not just a means to provide financial protection for your loved ones in the event of your passing; it can also serve as a powerful tool for wealth transfer. By incorporating life insurance into your estate planning, you can ensure that your hard-earned assets are passed down to your chosen beneficiaries efficiently and effectively. In this subchapter, we will explore various wealth transfer strategies using life insurance that can benefit both men and women.

One popular strategy is to use life insurance to equalize an inheritance among multiple beneficiaries. For instance, if you have a family business that you want to pass down to one child, but you also want to ensure that your other children receive an equal share of your estate, life insurance can bridge this gap. By naming the child who will inherit the business as the beneficiary of the policy, you can provide a fair inheritance to your other children by designating them as beneficiaries of the life insurance proceeds.

Another wealth transfer strategy is to use life insurance to cover estate taxes. In many cases, the value of an individual's estate may exceed the tax exemption limit, resulting in a hefty tax burden for their heirs. By purchasing a life insurance policy with a death benefit equal to the estimated tax liability, you can ensure that your loved ones are not burdened with the financial strain of paying estate taxes. This strategy can help preserve the value of your estate and ensure that your beneficiaries receive the full benefit of your hard work.

Furthermore, life insurance can be used to create a charitable legacy. If you have philanthropic goals, you can use life insurance to leave a significant donation to a charitable organization upon your passing. By naming the charity as the beneficiary of the policy, you can make a lasting impact and support causes that are important to you.

For those concerned about the cost of life insurance, it is worth mentioning that there are various types of policies available, such as term life insurance, whole life insurance, burial insurance, and final expense insurance. Each type offers different benefits and caters to specific needs. Term life insurance provides coverage for a specified period, while whole life insurance offers lifelong protection with the added benefit of accumulating cash value. Burial insurance and final expense insurance are specifically designed to cover funeral and end-of-life expenses. By understanding the different options, you can choose the policy that best aligns with your wealth transfer goals.

In conclusion, life insurance is a versatile tool that can be used to facilitate wealth transfer. Whether you want to equalize an inheritance, cover estate taxes, or create a charitable legacy, life insurance provides a solution. By considering the various types of life insurance policies available, you can tailor your wealth transfer strategy to fit your specific needs and ensure a secure future for your loved ones.

Ensuring a Lasting Legacy with Life Insurance

When it comes to securing your legacy and providing financial stability for your loved ones, life insurance is an invaluable tool that should not be overlooked. Whether you are a man or a woman, life insurance offers a range of options that can cater to your specific needs. In this subchapter, we will explore the various types of life insurance available, including term life insurance, whole life insurance, burial insurance, and final expense insurance.

Term life insurance is a popular option for those seeking temporary coverage at an affordable rate. It provides a death benefit to your beneficiaries for a specific period, typically ranging from 10 to 30 years. This type of policy is ideal for individuals who want to ensure their loved ones are financially protected during their working years or while paying off a mortgage or other debts.

On the other hand, whole life insurance provides lifelong coverage and accumulates cash value over time. This type of policy not only guarantees a death benefit but also serves as an investment vehicle. It offers the opportunity to build wealth and access funds for various purposes, such as education expenses or retirement planning.

Burial insurance, also known as final expense insurance, is specifically designed to cover funeral and burial expenses. This type of policy is ideal for individuals who want to alleviate the financial burden on their loved ones during a difficult time. It provides a modest death benefit that can be used to cover funeral costs, outstanding medical bills, or any other final expenses.

Regardless of the type of life insurance you choose, it is crucial to consider the long-term financial impact on your loved ones. Life insurance can provide financial security, replace lost income, pay off debts, and even fund a college education for your children. It ensures that your legacy lives on, even after you are gone.

When selecting a life insurance policy, it is essential to assess your financial goals, consider your current and future needs, and carefully evaluate the coverage options available. Consulting with a trusted financial advisor or insurance professional can help you navigate through the complexities of life insurance and make an informed decision.

In conclusion, life insurance is a powerful tool that enables you to secure your legacy and protect your loved ones financially. Regardless of your gender or specific needs, life insurance offers a range of options, including term life insurance, whole life insurance, burial insurance, and final expense insurance. By carefully considering your goals and consulting with professionals, you can ensure a lasting legacy that provides peace of mind and financial stability for generations to come.

Chapter 8: Choosing the Right Life Insurance Provider

Factors to Consider When Selecting a Life Insurance Provider

Choosing a life insurance provider is a crucial decision that can have a significant impact on your financial security and the well-being of your loved ones. With numerous options available in the market, it is essential to consider several factors to ensure you make an informed choice. This subchapter will guide you through the key factors to consider when selecting a life insurance provider, helping both men and women navigate the complex world of life insurance, including term life insurance, whole life insurance, burial insurance, and final expense insurance.

1. Financial Stability: The financial strength of an insurance company is paramount. Look for providers with a solid reputation and high ratings from independent rating agencies. This indicates their ability to honor claims and provide financial support when it matters most.

2. Policy Options: Consider the range of policies offered by each provider. Depending on your needs, you may require term life insurance, which offers coverage for a specified period, or whole life insurance, which provides lifelong protection and builds cash value over time. Additionally, burial insurance and final expense insurance can help cover funeral costs and other end-of-life expenses.

3. Pricing: Compare premiums and consider the affordability of the policy. Look for providers that offer competitive rates, ensuring that the coverage aligns with your budget. However, be cautious of policies that seem too good to be true, as they may have hidden costs or inadequate coverage.

4. Customer Service: Evaluate the level of customer service provided by the insurance company. Do they have a responsive and knowledgeable support team? Are they easily accessible in case you have questions or need assistance? Excellent customer service is crucial when dealing with the complexities of life insurance.

5. Reputation and Reviews: Research the reputation of the insurance provider by reading customer reviews and testimonials. This will give you insights into the experiences of others who have dealt with the company, helping you make an informed decision.

6. Claims Process: Consider the efficiency and effectiveness of the claims process. Look for a provider known for their smooth claims settlement and timely payouts, as this ensures your beneficiaries will receive the financial support they need without unnecessary delays.

By carefully considering these factors, both men and women can confidently select a life insurance provider that meets their unique needs. Whether you are looking for term life insurance, whole life insurance, burial insurance, or final expense insurance, understanding these factors will help you secure your legacy and provide financial security for your loved ones in the face of life's uncertainties.

Researching and Comparing Life Insurance Companies

When it comes to securing your legacy and protecting the financial well-being of your loved ones, choosing the right life insurance company is crucial. With the myriad of options available in the market, it is essential to conduct thorough research and comparisons to ensure you make an informed decision. This subchapter will guide you through the process of researching and comparing life insurance companies, enabling you to find the best fit for your needs.

Firstly, it is important to understand the different types of life insurance available. Whether you are considering term life insurance, whole life insurance, burial insurance, or final expense insurance, each type has its own unique features and benefits. By familiarizing yourself with the specifics of each policy, you can better assess which type aligns with your long-term goals and financial situation.

Once you have identified the type of life insurance that suits you, the next step is to research potential insurance companies. Start by looking for reputable and financially stable companies with a strong track record and positive customer reviews. Investigate factors such as the company's financial strength, customer service, claims process, and the range of policy options they offer. Additionally, consider the company's history and reputation within the industry, as well as any industry awards or recognitions they have received.

Comparing life insurance companies involves obtaining quotes and evaluating the cost and coverage provided. Request quotes from multiple companies, ensuring that you provide accurate and consistent information to enable a fair comparison. Compare not only the premiums but also any additional fees, riders, or benefits offered by each policy. It is important to strike a balance between affordability and the level of coverage provided.

In addition to cost, consider the company's underwriting process and eligibility requirements. Some companies may have stricter underwriting guidelines, which could impact your ability to obtain coverage. Moreover, evaluate the company's customer support and accessibility. A life insurance company that offers excellent customer service and clear communication channels can provide peace of mind throughout the policy term.

Lastly, seek recommendations and advice from trusted financial advisors or insurance professionals. They can provide insights based on their expertise and experience, helping you navigate the complexities of the life insurance market. By leveraging their knowledge, you can make a well-informed decision that aligns with your unique needs and goals.

In conclusion, researching and comparing life insurance companies is a crucial step in securing your legacy and protecting your loved ones' financial future. By understanding the different types of life insurance, researching potential companies, and comparing quotes and coverage, you can make a confident decision that provides the necessary protection and peace of mind for both men and women in various life insurance niches.

Evaluating Customer Service and Financial Stability

When it comes to securing your legacy and protecting your loved ones, choosing the right life insurance policy is crucial. With several options available in the market, it is essential to evaluate both customer service and financial stability of insurance providers. This subchapter will guide men and women, interested in life insurance, term life insurance, whole life insurance, burial insurance, and final expense insurance, on how to assess these vital factors.

Customer service plays a significant role in ensuring a seamless experience throughout the policy's duration. A reliable insurance provider should have a responsive and knowledgeable customer service team that can address your concerns and provide timely assistance. Look for positive reviews and testimonials from policyholders to gauge the company's commitment to customer satisfaction.

Financial stability is another crucial aspect to consider. You want to ensure that your chosen insurance company has the financial strength to meet its obligations when the time comes. Seek out providers with high ratings from reputable credit rating agencies such as A.M. Best, Standard & Poor's, or Moody's. These ratings reflect the company's ability to honor claims and remain financially stable in the long run.

Additionally, researching the company's history and longevity in the industry can provide insights into its stability. A well-established insurance provider with a long track record is generally a safer choice. Look for indicators of consistent growth and a strong financial foundation.

When evaluating customer service and financial stability, it is also beneficial to compare quotes from multiple insurance providers. Take the time to examine the coverage, benefits, and limitations of each policy. Consider factors such as premium rates, payout options, and any additional riders that may be available.

Don't hesitate to reach out to insurance agents or brokers specializing in life insurance. These professionals can help you navigate through various policies, explain complex terms, and provide personalized advice based on your specific needs.

Remember, securing your legacy is not just about obtaining a life insurance policy; it's about finding a trustworthy partner that will be there for your loved ones in their time of need. By evaluating customer service and financial stability, you can make an informed decision and gain peace of mind knowing that you have chosen a reliable insurance provider.

In the next section, we will delve deeper into the different types of life insurance policies available and discuss their respective benefits and suitability for various situations.

Questions to Ask Potential Life Insurance Providers

When it comes to securing your legacy and protecting your loved ones, life insurance is an essential tool that shouldn't be overlooked. Whether you're considering life insurance for the first time or looking to switch providers, asking the right questions can help you make an informed decision. Here are some key questions to ask potential life insurance providers:

1. What types of life insurance do you offer? - Understanding the different types of life insurance, such as term life insurance, whole life insurance, burial insurance, and final expense insurance, will

help you determine which option best suits your needs and financial goals.

2. How much coverage do I need? - Every individual's circumstances are unique, therefore it's crucial to assess your financial obligations and future needs. A reliable life insurance provider should be able to guide you through this process and help determine the appropriate coverage amount for your situation.

3. What are the premium costs? - Life insurance premiums can vary depending on factors such as age, health, and the type of coverage chosen. Request a detailed breakdown of costs to ensure it aligns with your budget and financial capabilities.

4. Can I customize my policy? - Flexibility is key when it comes to life insurance. Inquire about the ability to customize your policy to accommodate changes in your life or specific needs, ensuring your coverage remains relevant and adequate.

5. How do you determine underwriting? - Understanding the underwriting process is essential. Inquire about the factors that affect your underwriting, such as medical exams, health history, and lifestyle choices, to ensure you receive a fair and accurate assessment.

6. Are there any exclusions or limitations? - It's crucial to be aware of any exclusions or limitations

that may impact your coverage. Ask for a clear explanation of what is and isn't covered by the policy, including situations like suicide, risky hobbies, or pre-existing conditions.

7. What happens if I miss premium payments? - Life can be unpredictable, and it's important to know how missed premium payments will affect your coverage. Ask about the grace period, any penalties or fees, and if there are options to reinstate the policy if it lapses.

Remember, choosing a life insurance provider is a significant decision that can have a lasting impact on your financial security and the well-being of your loved ones. By asking these important questions, you can ensure that you find the right life insurance provider that aligns with your needs and goals, providing you with peace of mind and securing your legacy for generations to come.

Chapter 9: Life Insurance for Men

Unique Considerations for Men When Purchasing Life Insurance

When it comes to securing your legacy and protecting your loved ones, life insurance is an essential tool that every man should consider. However, there are some unique considerations that men need to keep in mind when purchasing life insurance. In this subchapter, we will delve into these considerations and shed light on the various options available to men in the realm of life insurance.

One of the key factors that men need to consider is their life expectancy. Statistics show that men generally have a shorter life expectancy compared to women. This means that men may face higher premiums when purchasing life insurance. However, there are ways to mitigate this issue. For instance, maintaining a healthy lifestyle, such as exercising regularly and eating a balanced diet, can positively impact your life insurance premiums.

Another important consideration for men is their occupation and hobbies. Certain jobs and hobbies may be considered high-risk by insurance companies, which can result in higher premiums or even exclusions in coverage. Men engaged in hazardous occupations or extreme sports should carefully review their policy terms to ensure that they are adequately covered.

Additionally, men need to take into account their roles as breadwinners and financial providers for their families. Life insurance can provide a safety net for your loved ones in the event of your untimely demise, ensuring that they are financially secure. It's crucial to accurately assess your family's financial needs, including ongoing expenses, debts, and future goals, when determining the coverage amount.

For men seeking life insurance, there are several options available, including term life insurance, whole life insurance, burial insurance, and final expense insurance. Each type of insurance has its own unique features and benefits, catering to different needs and financial situations. Understanding these options and working with an experienced insurance agent can help you make an informed decision that suits your specific circumstances.

In conclusion, men face specific considerations when purchasing life insurance. Understanding factors such as life expectancy, occupation, and family financial needs can help men make the right choices when selecting a policy. By considering these unique factors and exploring the various types of life insurance available, men can ensure that their loved ones are protected and their legacy is secured.

Life Insurance Options for Men at Different Life Stages

Life insurance is an essential tool for securing your family's financial future and providing peace of mind. However, the life insurance needs of men can vary depending on their life stage. Whether you are a young bachelor, a married man with children, or a senior looking to leave a legacy, it is crucial to understand the various life insurance options available to you. In this subchapter, we will explore the different life insurance options for men at different life stages.

For young bachelors, term life insurance can be an excellent choice. It offers coverage for a specific period, typically 10, 20, or 30 years, while keeping premiums affordable. This type of policy can provide financial support to your loved ones in the event of an untimely death and can be especially beneficial if you have student loans, credit card debt, or other financial obligations.

For married men with dependents, whole life insurance is a popular option. It provides lifelong coverage and builds cash value over time. This type of policy can help protect your family's financial security, pay off debts, and provide an inheritance for your loved ones. Additionally, whole life insurance can serve as a valuable asset for retirement planning, offering opportunities for tax-deferred growth.

For men in their senior years, burial insurance or final expense insurance can be vital. These policies are designed to cover funeral expenses, medical bills, and any outstanding debts. Burial insurance is typically easier to obtain and requires no medical exam, making it an attractive option for older individuals. Final expense insurance can also provide additional funds to cover any remaining financial obligations.

It is important to note that the above options are not mutually exclusive. Depending on your specific needs, you can combine different types of life insurance policies to create a comprehensive coverage plan. Consulting with a licensed insurance professional can help you determine the right mix of policies to meet your unique circumstances.

In conclusion, life insurance is a critical component of financial planning for men at different life stages. Whether you are young and single, married with a family, or a senior looking to leave a legacy, there are various life insurance options available to suit your needs. Understanding these options and working with a knowledgeable advisor can ensure that you secure your legacy and provide financial protection for your loved ones.

How Life Insurance Can Protect Men's Financial Future

Life is uncertain, and as men, we have a responsibility to protect our loved ones and secure their financial future. One of the most effective ways to do this is through life insurance. In this subchapter, we will explore how life insurance can safeguard your financial legacy and provide peace of mind for both men and women.

Life insurance comes in various forms, including term life insurance, whole life insurance, burial insurance, and final expense insurance. Each type has its own unique benefits, ensuring that you can choose the one that best suits your specific needs.

Term life insurance offers coverage for a specific period, such as 10, 20, or 30 years. It provides a death benefit to your beneficiaries if you pass away within the policy term. This type of insurance is particularly beneficial for men who have dependents, such as a spouse and children, as it ensures that they are financially protected during their most vulnerable years.

On the other hand, whole life insurance provides lifetime coverage and builds cash value over time. This type of insurance is an excellent choice for men who want to create a long-term financial plan and leave a legacy for their loved ones. With whole life insurance, you can enjoy the dual benefits of protection and investment.

Burial insurance and final expense insurance are specifically designed to cover end-of-life expenses. These policies ensure that funeral costs, medical bills, and other outstanding debts are taken care of, relieving your loved ones from the burden of financial stress during an already difficult time.

Regardless of the type of life insurance you choose, the key advantage is the financial security it provides. Life insurance can replace lost income, pay off debts, cover mortgage payments, fund your children's education, and even maintain your family's current lifestyle in your absence.

Moreover, life insurance can also be a valuable tool for estate planning and tax mitigation. It allows you to transfer wealth to future generations in a tax-efficient manner, ensuring that your hard-earned assets are preserved for your loved ones.

In conclusion, life insurance is an essential component of a comprehensive financial plan for men and women alike. It offers unparalleled protection, peace of mind, and financial security for your loved ones. By understanding the various types of life insurance and selecting the one that aligns with your goals and needs, you can secure your legacy and leave behind a lasting financial foundation for future generations.

Chapter 10: Life Insurance for Women

Unique Considerations for Women When Purchasing Life Insurance

When it comes to purchasing life insurance, both men and women have specific factors to consider. However, women face some unique considerations that can significantly impact their decision-making process. In this subchapter, we will explore the essential factors that women should keep in mind when purchasing life insurance.

One crucial consideration for women is their life expectancy. Statistics show that women tend to live longer than men, which means they may require coverage for a more extended period. It is essential to calculate the estimated length of coverage needed to ensure that your policy adequately protects you and your loved ones.

Another aspect to consider is the impact of pregnancy on life insurance. Women who are planning to start a family or are already pregnant should evaluate their coverage needs carefully. Life insurance can provide financial security for your child in case something unfortunate happens. It is advisable to review your policy and increase the coverage amount to consider the future needs of your growing family.

Furthermore, women often face unique health challenges throughout their lives, including pregnancy-related complications and certain illnesses. It is crucial to disclose any pre-existing medical conditions or family history of diseases when applying for life insurance. Some insurers offer policies tailored specifically to women's health concerns, such as breast cancer or reproductive health coverage. Understanding these options and selecting the right policy can ensure that your health needs are adequately addressed.

Additionally, women who are the primary caregivers or stay-at-home parents should also consider life insurance. While they may not have a direct income, their contributions are invaluable. If something were to happen to them, the surviving spouse would need financial assistance to cover childcare, household expenses, and other responsibilities. A life insurance policy can provide the necessary financial support to ensure that the family's needs are met.

Lastly, women should also evaluate their financial goals and long-term plans when purchasing life insurance. Whether it's saving for retirement, funding a child's education, or paying off debts, having a clear understanding of your financial objectives will help you determine the appropriate coverage amount and type of policy.

In conclusion, when purchasing life insurance, women should consider their longer life expectancy, pregnancy, unique health challenges, caregiving roles, and financial goals. By taking these factors into account, women can select a policy that provides comprehensive coverage and peace of mind for themselves and their loved ones.

Life Insurance Options for Women at Different Life Stages

Life insurance is a crucial financial tool that provides protection and peace of mind for individuals and their loved ones. Women, just like men, have unique life insurance needs that evolve as they pass through different stages of life. Understanding these needs and exploring the various life insurance options available can help women secure their legacy and protect their families.

For young women starting their careers or families, term life insurance is an excellent option. Term life insurance provides coverage for a specified period, typically ranging from 10 to 30 years. This coverage can help replace lost income, pay off debts, and cover childcare expenses in the event of an untimely death. Term life insurance is often affordable and offers high coverage amounts, making it an ideal choice for those with young families or significant financial obligations.

As women progress in their careers and accumulate assets, whole life insurance becomes a valuable consideration. Unlike term life insurance, whole life insurance provides lifelong coverage and builds cash value over time. This cash value can be used for various purposes, such as supplementing retirement income or funding educational expenses for children. Whole life insurance also offers the advantage of guaranteed death benefits, ensuring financial security for loved ones even in the face of market fluctuations.

For women in their later years, burial insurance or final expense insurance can be a practical solution. These types of insurance policies are designed to cover funeral and burial costs, as well as any outstanding debts or medical expenses. Burial insurance provides a small death benefit, typically ranging from $5,000 to $25,000, making it an affordable and manageable option for older women.

Regardless of the life stage, women should consider their unique circumstances when choosing a life insurance policy. Factors such as marital status, dependents, and financial responsibilities all play a role in determining the appropriate coverage amount and type of policy.

In conclusion, life insurance is essential for women at every stage of life. Whether it is term life insurance for young families, whole life insurance for asset accumulation, or burial insurance for later years, there are various options available to meet the specific needs of women. By securing the right life insurance policy, women can ensure their legacy and provide financial protection for their loved ones, regardless of what life may bring.

How Life Insurance Can Empower Women Financially

In today's world, women are taking charge of their lives and making significant strides in various fields. However, one area where women often lag behind is financial planning and security. Many women overlook the importance of life insurance, assuming it is a burden or unnecessary expense. However, life insurance can be a powerful tool for empowering women financially and providing them and their loved ones with a secure future.

Life insurance offers women a sense of financial security and peace of mind. It ensures that in the event of an untimely death, their loved ones are protected from the financial burden that can arise. Whether a woman is the primary breadwinner or a stay-at-home mom, life insurance provides a safety net for her family's future, allowing them to maintain their lifestyle, pay off debts, and cover expenses such as education and mortgage payments.

For single women, life insurance can also be a vital asset. It can serve as a means to leave a lasting legacy or support charitable causes close to their hearts. By including life insurance in their financial plans, single women can empower themselves by securing their financial legacy and ensuring their values are carried forward.

Moreover, life insurance can be particularly beneficial for women entrepreneurs and business owners. It can safeguard their businesses by providing funds to cover expenses, repay debts, and protect their partners or investors. Life insurance can also be used as collateral for business loans, helping women access capital to grow their ventures.

When it comes to life insurance, women should consider their unique needs and circumstances. Term life insurance offers affordable coverage for a specific period, making it ideal for young professionals or those with temporary financial obligations. On the other hand, whole life insurance provides lifelong coverage and an investment component, allowing women to build cash value over time.

Burial insurance and final expense insurance are also important considerations for women. These policies provide coverage specifically for funeral and end-of-life expenses, relieving loved ones of the financial burden during a difficult time.

In conclusion, life insurance is a powerful tool that can empower women financially. It provides a safety net for their loved ones, allows them to leave a lasting legacy, protects their businesses, and ensures financial security throughout their lives. By understanding the different types of life insurance and considering their unique needs, women can take control of their financial futures and secure their legacies.

Chapter 11: Securing Your Legacy

Steps to Take When Securing Your Legacy with Life Insurance

When it comes to securing your legacy, life insurance is an invaluable tool that can provide financial protection and peace of mind for both men and women. Whether you are considering life insurance, term life insurance, whole life insurance, burial insurance, or final expense insurance, taking the following steps can help you make informed decisions and ensure that your loved ones are taken care of in the future.

1. Assess your needs: Begin by evaluating your financial situation, current obligations, and future goals. Consider factors such as mortgage payments, outstanding debts, education expenses, and the standard of living you want to provide for your

family. This assessment will help you determine the appropriate coverage amount and type of life insurance that suits your needs.

2. Research different types of life insurance: Familiarize yourself with the various options available, such as term life insurance, whole life insurance, burial insurance, and final expense insurance. Each type offers different benefits and features, so understanding them will empower you to make an informed choice that aligns with your goals.

3. Seek professional advice: Consult with a reputable life insurance agent or financial advisor who specializes in life insurance. They can guide you through the process, provide personalized recommendations, and answer any questions you may have. Their expertise will ensure that you select the right policy and coverage for your unique circumstances.

4. Compare quotes and policies: Obtain quotes from multiple insurance providers and compare their offerings. Pay attention to factors such as premiums, coverage limits, policy terms, and any additional benefits or riders. This comparison will enable you to find the most cost-effective and comprehensive policy that meets your requirements.

5. Review the policy details: Before finalizing your decision, carefully review the terms and conditions of the policy. Understand any exclusions, limitations, or waiting periods that may apply. Ensure that the policy aligns with your expectations and covers all the necessary aspects of your financial plan.

6. Regularly review and update your policy: Life insurance should not be a set-it-and-forget-it aspect of your financial plan. As your circumstances change over time, it is important to review and update your policy accordingly. Marriage, having children, purchasing a home, or starting a business are all events that may require adjustments to your coverage.

By following these steps, you can navigate the process of securing your legacy with life insurance. Taking the time to evaluate your needs, educate yourself on different policy types, seek professional advice, compare quotes, and regularly review your policy will ensure that you have the right coverage in place to protect your loved ones and leave a lasting legacy.

Reviewing and Updating Your Life Insurance Policy Regularly

One of the most crucial aspects of owning a life insurance policy is to review and update it regularly. Life is constantly changing, and your insurance coverage should reflect those changes to ensure that your loved ones are adequately protected in the event of your passing. In this subchapter, we will delve into the importance of reviewing and updating your life insurance policy regularly, regardless of the type of coverage you have.

Life insurance is not a set-and-forget type of investment. As men and women, we experience various milestones and life events that can impact our insurance needs. Whether you have a term life insurance, whole life insurance, burial insurance, or final expense insurance policy, keeping it up to date is vital.

Regularly reviewing your policy allows you to assess any changes in your financial situation, family dynamics, or personal goals. For instance, if you recently got married or had a child, you may want to increase your coverage to provide more financial security for your growing family. On the other hand, if your children have become financially independent, you might consider reducing your coverage to reflect your changing responsibilities.

Furthermore, reviewing your life insurance policy regularly enables you to evaluate its performance against your financial objectives. As the market evolves, so do the available insurance products and pricing options. By staying informed about the latest trends and offerings, you can determine if your current policy is still the most suitable one for your needs. This practice may also present opportunities to secure better rates or enhanced coverage that aligns with your current circumstances.

Beyond personal changes, legislative updates and tax laws can also impact your life insurance policy. Regularly reviewing your coverage allows you to stay abreast of any legal changes that may affect your policy and make any necessary adjustments to remain compliant.

In conclusion, reviewing and updating your life insurance policy regularly is a fundamental step towards securing your legacy. As men and women, we must recognize that our insurance needs change over time, and keeping our policies up to date ensures that our loved ones are protected and financially secure. Whether you have life insurance, term life insurance, whole life insurance, burial insurance, or final expense insurance, taking the time to review and update your policy is an investment in your family's future.

Working with Professionals to Optimize Your Life Insurance Strategy

When it comes to securing your legacy and protecting your loved ones, having a comprehensive life insurance strategy is crucial. However, navigating the complex world of life insurance can be overwhelming, especially with the variety of options available. That's why working with professionals who specialize in life insurance can make a significant difference in optimizing your strategy.

Life insurance professionals are knowledgeable experts who understand the intricacies of different policies and can guide you through the process of selecting the right one for your specific needs. Whether you're considering term life insurance, whole life insurance, burial insurance, or final expense insurance, these professionals can offer valuable insights and help you make informed decisions.

One of the primary advantages of working with professionals is their ability to assess your unique circumstances and financial goals. They will take into account factors such as your age, health, income, and family situation to determine the most suitable policy for you. By conducting a thorough analysis, they can identify any coverage gaps or potential risks that may arise in the future.

Another benefit of collaborating with professionals is their access to a wide range of insurance providers. Instead of spending countless hours researching and comparing policies on your own, these experts can present you with multiple options from reputable companies. They can explain the pros and cons of each policy, ensuring you understand what you're signing up for and helping you find the best coverage at the most affordable rates.

Furthermore, life insurance professionals can assist you in evaluating your existing policy, making adjustments, or even finding alternatives that better align with your evolving needs. They can help you understand the policy's terms and conditions, including any exclusions or limitations, and advise you on potential riders or additional coverage options that might enhance your policy.

Ultimately, working with professionals can save you time, money, and unnecessary stress. They will simplify the complex jargon associated with life insurance, empowering you to make well-informed decisions that align with your long-term goals. By optimizing your life insurance strategy, you can ensure that your loved ones are adequately protected and that your legacy remains intact.

Whether you're a man or a woman, and regardless of whether you're looking for life insurance, term life insurance, whole life insurance, burial insurance, or final expense insurance, consider enlisting the expertise of professionals to guide you through this crucial process. Their knowledge and experience will be invaluable in securing the best possible coverage for you and your loved ones. Remember, your legacy deserves the utmost protection, and professionals can help you achieve just that.

Celebrating Your Legacy and Ensuring Peace of Mind

In this subchapter, we will explore the importance of celebrating your legacy and how life insurance can play a significant role in securing your family's future. Whether you are a man or a woman, life insurance is a crucial financial tool that provides protection and peace of mind for both you and your loved ones.

Life insurance is not just about having a safety net in case of unexpected events; it is an opportunity to celebrate your accomplishments and ensure a lasting impact on the people and causes you care about. By creating a comprehensive life insurance plan, you can leave a legacy that reflects your values and aspirations.

One of the most common types of life insurance is term life insurance. This type of policy provides coverage for a specific period, typically 10, 20, or even 30 years. Term life insurance is an excellent option for those who want affordable coverage during their working years to protect their income, mortgage, and education expenses for their children.

For those seeking lifelong protection, whole life insurance is an ideal choice. This type of policy offers coverage for the entire duration of your life, as long as premiums are paid. Whole life insurance not only provides a death benefit but also builds cash value over time, which can be utilized for various financial needs such as education funding, retirement planning, or emergencies.

Burial insurance and final expense insurance are niche products specifically designed to cover funeral and burial costs. These policies ensure that your loved ones are not burdened with the financial stress of arranging a proper farewell. By securing burial or final expense insurance, you can celebrate your legacy by providing a dignified and respectful farewell for your family and friends.

Regardless of the life insurance policy you choose, it is essential to regularly review and update the coverage to align with your changing circumstances. Life events such as marriage, the birth of a child, or the purchase of a new home may require adjustments to your policy to ensure adequate protection.

In conclusion, celebrating your legacy and ensuring peace of mind go hand in hand when it comes to life insurance. By creating a comprehensive plan that reflects your values and aspirations, you can leave a lasting impact on your loved ones and the causes you hold dear. Whether it's term life insurance, whole life insurance, burial insurance, or final expense insurance, there is a policy tailored to your unique needs. Take control of your legacy today and secure a brighter future for yourself and those you care about.

Chapter 12: Frequently Asked Questions about Life Insurance

Common Questions about Life Insurance

Life insurance is a vital financial tool that provides protection and peace of mind for both men and women. In this subchapter, we will address some of the most common questions about life insurance to help you make informed decisions about your financial future. Whether you are considering life insurance, term life insurance, whole life insurance, burial insurance, or final expense insurance, this information will be invaluable.

1. What is life insurance?
Life insurance is a contract between you and an insurance company. In exchange for regular

premium payments, the insurance company guarantees a sum of money, known as a death benefit, to be paid to your beneficiaries upon your death. This benefit can be used to cover various expenses, including funeral costs, debt payments, and ongoing financial support for your loved ones.

2. What is the difference between term life insurance and whole life insurance?
Term life insurance provides coverage for a specific period, typically 10, 20, or 30 years. It is more affordable and offers a higher death benefit. Whole life insurance, on the other hand, provides coverage for your entire life and accumulates cash value over time. It offers lifelong protection and can serve as an investment vehicle.

3. Who should consider burial insurance and final expense insurance?
Burial insurance and final expense insurance are designed to cover the costs associated with funerals and other end-of-life expenses. These types of insurance are ideal for individuals who want to ensure that their loved ones are not burdened with financial obligations after their passing.

4. How much life insurance coverage do I need?
The amount of life insurance coverage you need depends on various factors, including your age, income, debts, and financial goals. It is recommended to calculate your long-term financial

needs, such as mortgage payments, education expenses, and income replacement, to determine an appropriate coverage amount.

5. Can I change my life insurance policy?
Yes, life insurance policies can be modified to meet your changing needs. You can increase or decrease your coverage, convert term life insurance to whole life insurance, or add additional riders to customize your policy.

Remember, life insurance is not a one-size-fits-all solution. It is essential to consult with a licensed insurance professional to assess your unique circumstances and determine the best life insurance policy for you. By understanding these common questions about life insurance, you can make informed decisions to secure your legacy and provide financial protection for your loved ones.

Clarifying Misconceptions and Myths Surrounding Life Insurance

Life insurance is a crucial financial tool that provides protection and peace of mind to individuals and their loved ones. However, there are many misconceptions and myths surrounding life insurance that often lead to confusion. In this subchapter, we aim to debunk these misconceptions and shed light on the importance of life insurance for men and women.

One common misconception is that life insurance is only necessary for those with dependents or young families. While it is true that life insurance plays a vital role in providing financial support for dependents, it is not limited to this purpose. Life insurance can also be beneficial for single individuals, empty nesters, and retirees. It can provide an inheritance, cover funeral expenses, or even serve as a source of supplemental income during retirement.

Another prevalent myth is that life insurance is too expensive and only for the affluent. The truth is that life insurance comes in various types and coverage amounts, allowing individuals to find a policy that suits their budget and needs. Term life insurance, for example, offers affordable coverage for a specific period, while whole life insurance provides lifelong coverage with a cash value component. There are also burial insurance and final expense insurance options specifically designed to cover end-of-life expenses.

Furthermore, some people believe that life insurance is unnecessary if they have enough savings or investments. While having savings is important, life insurance offers a level of protection that savings alone cannot provide. It ensures that your loved ones are financially secure in the event of your untimely passing and can help cover debts, mortgage payments, education expenses, and other financial obligations.

It is also important to address the misconception that life insurance is only for older individuals. The reality is that the younger and healthier you are when you purchase a life insurance policy, the lower your premiums will be. By securing life insurance early, you can lock in a lower rate and provide financial security for your loved ones.

In conclusion, life insurance is a valuable tool that offers financial protection and peace of mind to individuals and their families. It is not limited to specific demographics, as it can benefit men and women in various stages of life. By clarifying these misconceptions and debunking myths, we hope to encourage individuals to explore the different types of life insurance available and make informed decisions that secure their legacy.

Tips for Making Informed Decisions about Life Insurance

Life insurance is an essential component of financial planning that ensures your loved ones are protected and financially secure even after you're gone. However, with the wide range of life insurance options available, it can be overwhelming to choose the right policy that meets your specific needs. In this subchapter, we will provide you with some valuable tips to make informed decisions about life insurance.

1. Assess Your Needs: Begin by assessing your financial situation and the needs of your dependents. Consider factors such as outstanding debts, mortgage, future education expenses, and income replacement. This evaluation will help you determine the appropriate coverage amount.

2. Understand the Types of Life Insurance: Familiarize yourself with the different types of life insurance policies available, such as term life insurance, whole life insurance, burial insurance, and final expense insurance. Each type has its own features, benefits, and drawbacks, so it's important to understand which one aligns with your goals and circumstances.

3. Research and Compare: Don't settle for the first life insurance policy you come across. Take the time to research and compare different insurers, their reputation, financial stability, and customer reviews. Make sure to request quotes from multiple providers to find the most suitable coverage at an affordable premium.

4. Seek Professional Advice: Life insurance can be a complex subject, and seeking advice from a licensed insurance agent or financial advisor can be immensely helpful. They can provide personalized

guidance based on your unique circumstances, ensuring you make an informed decision and avoid common pitfalls.

5. Review the Policy Details: Before finalizing a life insurance policy, carefully review the terms, conditions, and exclusions. Understand the policy's coverage period, premiums, renewal options, and any additional riders or benefits that may be available. Ensure the policy meets your specific requirements and offers the necessary flexibility.

6. Regularly Re-evaluate: Life circumstances change over time, so it's crucial to regularly reassess your life insurance needs. Major life events such as getting married, having children, or purchasing a new home might require adjustments to your coverage. Stay proactive and update your policy accordingly.

By following these tips, men and women can make well-informed decisions about life insurance. Remember, life insurance is not a one-size-fits-all solution, and it's essential to choose a policy that aligns with your unique needs and circumstances. Taking the time to understand your options and seeking professional advice will ensure you secure the right coverage to protect your loved ones and leave a lasting legacy.

Conclusion: Taking Control of Your Financial Future with Life Insurance

In this book, "Securing Your Legacy: A Guide to Life Insurance for Men and Women," we have explored the myriad benefits and options available to both men and women when it comes to life insurance. Whether you are considering life insurance for the first time or looking to reassess your current coverage, understanding the various types of policies and how they can positively impact your financial future is crucial.

Life insurance is not just a tool for providing financial protection to your loved ones in the event of your untimely passing; it is also a means to ensure your own financial security throughout your lifetime. By taking control of your financial future with life insurance, you can gain peace of mind knowing that you have a safety net in place to navigate life's uncertainties.

One of the most common forms of life insurance is term life insurance. This type of policy offers coverage for a specific period, typically 10, 20, or 30 years, and provides a death benefit to your beneficiaries if you pass away during the policy term. Term life insurance is an excellent choice for those seeking affordable coverage and temporary financial protection, such as paying off a mortgage or funding a child's education.

On the other hand, whole life insurance provides lifelong coverage and often includes a cash value component that grows over time. This cash value can be accessed during your lifetime and used for various purposes, such as supplementing retirement income or covering unexpected expenses. Whole life insurance is suitable for individuals seeking long-term financial stability and the ability to leave a legacy for future generations.

For those specifically looking for burial insurance or final expense insurance, there are specialized policies tailored to meet these needs. These types of policies are designed to cover funeral and burial costs, ensuring that your loved ones are not burdened with these expenses during their time of grief.

By taking the time to understand your unique financial goals and needs, you can choose the life insurance policy that aligns with your objectives. Life insurance is an investment in your future and the financial well-being of those you care about. It provides a safety net, allowing you to live your life to the fullest knowing that you have taken the necessary steps to protect your loved ones and secure your legacy.

In conclusion, life insurance is not just a financial product; it is a tool that empowers you to take control of your financial future. It provides peace of mind, knowing that you have a plan in place to protect your loved ones and ensure your own financial security. Whether you opt for term life insurance, whole life insurance, burial insurance, or final expense insurance, the key is to assess your needs, consult with a trusted advisor, and make an informed decision that will benefit you and your family for years to come. Take control of your financial future today by exploring the world of life insurance.

Do you have life insurance?

Life insurance statistics vary, covering aspects like coverage, demographics, and industry trends. As of my last knowledge update in January 2022, here are some general insights:

1. **Coverage Rates:**

   - In the United States, about 54% of individuals have life insurance coverage.

2. **Types of Policies:**

   - Term life insurance is popular, constituting around 60-70% of policies purchased.

3. **Age Demographics:**

 - Younger individuals (under 35) are less likely to have life insurance, with ownership increasing with age.

4. **Reasons for Purchase:**

 - Many people buy life insurance for family protection, mortgage coverage, and income replacement.

5. **Global Trends:**

 - The life insurance market globally is influenced by factors like economic conditions and regulatory changes.

Please note that these figures may have changed, and it's advisable to refer to the latest industry reports for the most up-to-date statistics. Anything specific you're curious about within life insurance statistics?9

Certainly! Life insurance ownership tends to vary across different age demographics:

1. **Young Adults (18-34):**

   - Typically, a lower percentage owns life insurance.

   - May start considering coverage as they begin families or acquire financial responsibilities.

2. **Middle-Aged Adults (35-54):**

   - Higher ownership rates, especially among those with dependents.

   - Considered a prime age for purchasing life insurance due to family and financial obligations.

3. **Seniors (55 and above):**

   - Ownership remains significant, often for estate planning or covering final expenses.

   - Some policies may have been purchased earlier in life and are maintained into retirement.

It's important to note that individual circumstances and priorities vary, influencing the age at which individuals choose to purchase life insurance. If you have a specific age group in mind or want more detailed information, feel free to specify!

The choice between term life and whole life insurance depends on your individual needs and financial goals. Here's a brief overview to help you decide:

1. **Term Life Insurance:**

   - **Purpose:** Provides coverage for a specific term (e.g., 10, 20, or 30 years).

   - **Cost:** Generally more affordable than whole life.

   - **Renewal:** Premiums may increase upon renewal.

   - **Cash Value:** Does not accumulate cash value.

   - **Suitable for:** Those seeking affordable coverage for a set period, like during mortgage years or while raising a family.

2. **Whole Life Insurance:**

- **Purpose:** Provides coverage for your entire life.

- **Cost:** Premiums are higher than term life.

- **Cash Value:** Builds cash value over time that can be accessed or borrowed against.

- **Lifetime Coverage:** No need for renewal, and premiums remain consistent.

- **Suitable for:** Individuals looking for lifelong coverage, estate planning, or an investment component.

The "best" policy depends on your specific situation, financial goals, and preferences. If you want pure protection for a specific period, term life may be suitable. If you want lifelong coverage with an investment component, whole life might be a better fit.

Consider consulting with a financial advisor to determine which aligns better with your overall financial plan. Is there a specific aspect you'd like more information on?

Life Insurance Stats at a Glance

- According to results from a Forbes Advisor survey on life insurance, at least three in four American adults have some form of life insurance.[1]
- Women (22%) are twice as likely as men (11%) to lack life insurance.[1]
- Forbes Advisor survey respondents were commonly unaware that certain aspects of personal history—unrelated to health—are considered by insurers when determining an individual's life insurance quote:
  - Only 35% of respondents knew that driving records are usually considered.
  - 33% knew criminal history could be considered.
  - 29% knew credit history could be considered.
  - 23% knew a current bankruptcy is often considered.[1]
- Almost 60% of respondents to a Forbes Advisor survey on marijuana and life insurance indicated they'd have reservations about applying for life insurance if they legally used marijuana.[2]
- More than half (56%) of respondents indicated they would not respond honestly to

questions about marijuana use in order to sidestep higher life insurance quotes.[2]

- Many Americans view life insurance as a means of protecting their families from unpaid debt. White respondents (64%) to a Forbes Advisor survey were much more likely to indicate this view than Black respondents (37%).[3]
- A relatively small number of Americans view life insurance as a means of passing down generational wealth. Black respondents (22%) were nearly three times as likely as white respondents (8%) to indicate this view.[3]
- Eight out of 10 consumers overestimate the expense of getting a life insurance policy, according to a study by LIMRA and Life Happens.[4]
- Fewer than half of people without life insurance surveyed in this study say they feel financially secure. The same survey found that 68% of life insurance owners say they do feel financially secure.[4]
- This feeling of financial security rises to 78% when a consumer has both employer-based and individual life insurance policies, according to the Insurance Information Institute.[5]

- The number of Americans who believe they don't have enough life insurance has more than doubled since 2010.[5]
- 44% of American households would encounter significant financial difficulties within half a year if they lost the primary wage earner in the family, and 28% would reach this point in only a month.[6]

www.ingramcontent.com/pod-product-compliance
Lightning Source LLC
Chambersburg PA
CBHW071053290526
45795CB00004B/1460